Have I ever told you...

Have I ever told you...

with illustrations by
Larry Adler

Delancey Press *dp* London 2001

Published by Delancey Press Ltd
4 Delancey Passage, London NW1 7NN
in association with
The Book Guild Limited
25 High Street, Lewes, East Sussex BN7 2LU
www.bookguild.co.uk

Some of the material in this book has appeared in *Jokes and
how to tell them* (Doubleday 1963), *It Ain't Necessarily So –
The autobiography of Larry Adler* (Collins 1984)

First published October 2001
Edited by T. von Saxe
Designed and typeset by Jonathan Sargent
Dust jacket incorporates a caricature of Larry Adler by NORKIN
Printed by W S Bookwell

ISBN 0-9539119-1-8

Contents

Introduction

I love to write. I also respect language and consider it a precious thing, being like liberty in demanding eternal vigilance. When I play music I know only one way to play: my best.

President Eisenhower once told me: "When someone comes to a meeting looking stiff and formal, I offer him a drink, crack a joke and in no time he's a human being." I love a good joke, detest a bad one, the latter including all stereotyped humour. If the point telegraphs itself, it isn't funny. I often tell jokes in lieu of conversation, as I find shared laughter a most important element in any relationship.

I know my mind is unorganised. I have always loved reading and I'm a purist about language. But I am also a procrastinator. I learned how to write music at the instigation of Ingrid Bergman. Her disapproval that I couldn't write music and her comment *"you seem to be proud of your ignorance"* were motivation enough! Had it not been for this I would never have dared to tackle a film score, probably would never have composed at all.

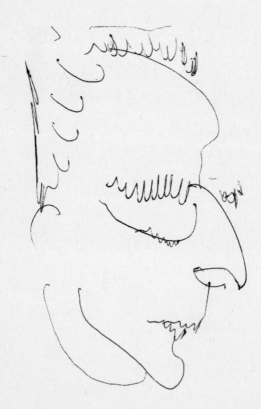

Have I ever told you...

I did several concerts with Marvin Hamlisch, Conductor of the Washington Philharmonic. I think the reason for this is because he seemed to like my jokes more than my music. He kept saying: "I wish I had said that"…

Telling jokes is one of my favourite pastimes. The only time when I'm unable to tell one is when I'm playing the "mouth organ".

Have I Ever Told You… is a compilation of the stories I like best. I would like to think that you will find them funny and interesting: an enjoyable glimpse into the nature of humour.

Larry Adler

Illustrations are all by Larry Adler unless credited otherwise.
Stick figures brought to life by the expression on their faces.

Jokes

Adam to Eve: "Do you *really* love me?"
Eve: "Who else?!"

Jokes

A very drunk man is walking with one foot on the road and the other on the pavement. A man stops him and tells him what he's doing. To this he replies: "Thank God. I thought I had gone lame."

A man from Poland comes to live with his brother in London. He speaks no English and his brother teaches him to say "Apple pie and coffee" so that at least he can get something for lunch. After a fortnight he begs his brother to teach him to say something else. The brother thinks for a while and says, "Okay, try this – chicken sandwich."

When he tells the waiter "Tsee-ken sond-weets", the next day, the waiter asks: "On what".

The fellow repeats: "Tsee-ken sond-weets."

"Okay, okay. I heard you the first time. How do you want it: on whole wheat, white or rye?"

(Gulp) "Opple pie and cawfee."

A zebra is walking down a country lane in England. She sees some sheep in a field, comes up to the fence and calls to one of them:

"Excuse me, could I speak to you for just a moment? I represent the United Women Zebras of South Africa. I'm here on a fact-finding tour, to find out how English animals live and work. Would you care to tell me just what it is that you do?"

The sheep says: "I give wool, what else? When I grow enough wool, they shear it off and next season it's the same routine again. Is it different in your country?"

"No, actually, quite the same. Well, thank you – you've been most kind."

Later on, farther down the road, she sees a cow.

"I beg your pardon, I'm from the United Women Zebras of South Africa. I've been delegated to interview English animals. Would you describe to me your function as an English cow?"

"Not at all, I'm glad you asked me that. I'm pure bred Guernsey, I give Grade A milk. All this pasture around here is for me and a few close friends. I live up there in that white barn – I'm sorry I can't ask you in but we're house-cleaning and the place is just a shambles."

"I see. Well thank you so much, you've been most helpful."

Later on she sees a stallion in a field. The stallion sees her, too. He comes charging toward the fence, comes to a four-footed skidding stop, and just looms over her with nostrils flaring. She looks up at him.

"And just what is it that *you* do?"

The stallion says, "Honey, you just slip out of that housecoat and I'll show you what I do!"

Jokes

Three women are discussing their sons:

"My boy, Leopold, is so loving and caring. Comes wintertime, he sends me for a fortnight to Miami Beach. He arranges everything and pays for everything. That is how much he thinks of me."

The second one says, "That's very nice, very nice indeed. But my Stanley not only *sends* me to Miami for two weeks but he *takes* me there and looks after me. That is how much he thinks of me."

The third mother says, "Well, you both have two fine boys there, no doubt about it. But my Irving – he goes every day, six days a week, to see a man; pays him fifty dollars each time and Irving lies down on a couch and talks. And do you know what he talks about? Me!"

Moses is leading the Jews through the desert. A man arrives on horseback.

"Moses, I've got bad news. The boss has changed his mind. He wants you all back in Egypt and he's sending his army for you."

Moses says, "Send for my P. R. man."

The P. R. man is told what the situation is.

"Look, Moses, baby. Tomorrow we get to the Red Sea. Right? Here's what I want you to do. You're gonna go to the banks of the Red Sea and you're gonna say, 'Waters, part.' And them waters are gonna part. Then we go through the channel and we wait on the other side. When them Gyppos come up, they see the channel we made and they start to go through it, see? Then, when they get to the middle, you're gonna say, 'Waters, come together,' and the waters come together, them Gyppos get drowned and we're quids in."

Moses says, "You think it will work?"

The P. R. man says. "I can't be absolutely sure. But if it does work, I guarantee you four pages in the Old Testament."

Jokes

A woman has her husband's body cremated and has the ashes put in an urn, which she puts on the piano in the living room. She doesn't tell her friends what it is and they get into the habit of tapping their cigarettes into it. One day, about six months later, she's doing some spring cleaning. She picks up the urn and says to her maid, "I know you're gonna think I'm crazy, but I could swear Sam is putting on weight."

Two horses in adjoining stalls at a racing stable. One horse says:

"Fred, I don't know if you've heard, but there's a rumour that I'm going to be sold. I haven't done too well my last few times out. I like it here and I would hate to leave. Now Fred – I don't quite know how to say this – it's very embarrassing – but it so happens we're both running in the same race tomorrow. Fred, if I could come in a winner for just that one race..."

The other horse says, "Bert, I sympathise with you. I would hate to see you go. But Bert, what you're suggesting – well, in a way, you're asking me to violate my own code of ethics as a race horse. Bert I'd do anything in the world for you but..."

A bulldog, lying at their feet, looks up and says, "Look, Fred, is it gonna kill you if Bert wins one race?"

One horse says, "Get a load of that – a *talking* dog!"

A chimpanzee comes into a bar, orders a martini and puts down a ten-pound note. The bartender goes back to the till and speaks to his boss who has been watching: "Hey, how 'bout that! He ordered a martini and gave me a tenner. What do you think?"

The boss says, "Aah, give him a pound change, see what happens. He probably won't know the difference."

The bartender serves the drink and puts down a pound change. He says to the chimp, "You new around here?"

The chimp says, "Yup."

"Yeh, I thought you were. You know, we don't get many chimpanzees comin' in here."

The chimp says, "At nine pounds for a martini, I'm not surprised."

Jokes

Two girls meet on the beach at Miami. One says:

"So what's new?"

The other says, "Wait'll you hear! I was at the doctor's this morning, he gives me an examination, and you know what he says? He says I'm gradually turning into a man."

"So what *else* is new?"

He: "I've given you the best years of my life."

She: "And who *made* them the best?"

He: "I've never taken a virgin home."
She: *"I'm* a virgin."
"You're not home yet."

Eve to Adam: "Are we black or are we white?"
Adam: "I don't know – go ask the Lord".
Eve to Adam: "The Lord said: You are what you are".
Adam: "We are white".
Eve: "Why?"
Adam: "Otherwise, He would have said: You is what you is."

Jokes

A man is in an accident and is bandaged from head to toe. When they are ready to take off the bandages he anxiously asks the nurse. "My hands, my fingers. Will I be able to play the piano?"

The nurse replies: "Of course you will – perfectly."

The patient says: "Well that will be amazing. I couldn't play the piano *before* the accident."

A woman coming out of hotel bumps into a man who says: "I beg your pardon – hey – you are the *ugliest* woman I've ever seen."
To which she replies: "You're drunk".
"Quite true. I'm very drunk. But tomorrow I'll be sober. And you'll still be the ugliest woman I've ever seen."

A burglar is trying to get into a house. He tries all the doors and windows but no success. Now he's up on the second floor balcony. He looks in and sees a baby in a crib. By now he's pretty desperate so he talks to the baby:

"Oo-oo, bay-bee," he says, "itsy-bitsy poo, isn't oo gonna open window for nice mansie-wansie, hmmm?"

"Ah, ya dumb bastard, I can't even *walk* yet!"

Jokes

A week old baby is talking and walking. The news team is interviewing him and asks if he knows how he was born.

"A product of the sexual relationship of my parents."

"Wow, you are only a week old and you know that already?"

"Of course. I wasn't born yesterday!"

On Christmas Eve, in London, a man is begging in the street. A fellow comes along, full of holiday spirit and hands the beggar a fifty pound note. The beggar looks at the bill, turns around and runs to a trendy brasserie. The man, surprised, follows him and sees the beggar with some gravad lax and a glass of champagne.

"You sonofabitch," says the man. "I give you fifty pounds, that's probably more than you've seen in a long time, and you go and blow it on gravad lax and champagne."

The beggar says, "Look, when I haven't got money, I can't eat gravad lax and drink champagne. When I've got money, I mustn't eat gravad lax and drink champagne. When *can* I eat gravad lax and drink champagne?"

Jokes

A man is praying in Church:
"God, please help me to get a Pound."
Another man arrives, kneels and asks:
"God, please help me to get a hundred thousand pounds for my property deal."
First man: "God, please, please. I need a Pound."
The second man gets up, goes to the first one and gives him a Pound.
He kneels down again and says: "Now God, if I may have Your *undivided* attention!"

A man tells his wife: "You're useless. You don't bring any money in to the house. Why don't you try being a prostitute." She goes out, comes back late that night with a bag full of dollars and one dime. He asks: "Who gave you a dime?" She replies: *"Everybody"*.

A man gets a job in a large corporation. First day on the job he asks an executive. "Hey, man, where's the water-cooler at?" The executive says, "When you work for our company you must learn *never* to end a sentence with a preposition." "Oh, I'm sorry… Allow me to re-phrase the question. Where's the water-cooler at, *asshole*?"

Jokes

In Court there are three girls charged with soliciting in the street and one man arrested for operating a pushcart without a licence. First one of the girls comes before the Judge.

"Your Honour," she says, "I was just walking along with my friend here when a man asked me did I have a match. Well, the next thing I knew, this officer appeared and *ooh*, the *things* he *said*! Perfectly *disgraceful*, and I mean, how anybody could even *think* such a thing..."

The Judge looks at the charge sheet.

"Chantal Galore," he says, "I find here that you've had three previous convictions for soliciting. I fine you fifty pounds or six days in jail. Next case."

The second girl says, "Your Honour, it's exactly like she says. We're both private secretaries, a perfectly *respectable* occupation and if our mothers ever so much as *dreamed* that we were in this court, they'd *die* of shame, they really *would*."

The Judge says, "Puzzy Gonore, you've had five previous convictions on the same charge – soliciting. That will be seventy pounds or ten days in jail. Next?"

The third girl says, "Judge, I am a whore. I'm not proud of it but that's what I am and that's about the only way for me to make a living."

"Young lady," the Judge says, "in all my years on the bench you're the first honest woman to come before this Court. Your case is dismissed. Oh, and Sergeant, make out a contribution for this young lady of fifty pounds from the Policemen's Fund. Next case?"

The old fellow arrested for operating a pushcart comes up.

"Your Honour," he says, "what's the use of trying to fool a learned man like you. I'm a whore."

Two fellows are mountain climbing and one falls about two thousand feet. His friend looks out over the precipice and yells:

"Seymour! Are you all right?"

"I'm fine but can't move my arms or legs. Otherwise I'm fine!"

"Seymour. I'm going to lower you a rope. Catch it in your teeth. I will haul you up!"

Finally Seymour is near the top.

"Ah, Seymour, it's good to see you, fella – how are you feeling?"

"I'm FI-II-ii..."

Jokes

One cannibal says to the other one. "I don't like my mother in law".
His friend tells him: "Just eat the vegetables."

Accused to Judge: "My Lord, as God
is my witness, I am not guilty."
Judge to accused: "He is not, I am,
you are."

A man passes a pet shop, hears a canary, comes into the shop and says he wants
to buy the bird. Just as the owner is about to wrap up the cage the man says:
  "Hey, wait a minute, I just noticed – that canary's only got one leg."
  The canary says: "Look, Mac, whaddya want – a singer or a dancer?"

A dying man detects a delicious smell coming
from the kitchen where a cake is being baked.
He asks his wife if he can have a piece – "Sam,
don't be silly. That's for *after* the funeral."

"Whatever made you think I was wicked?!"

"I'm wearing the yarmulke 'cos I'm tired of being taken for a W.A.S.P."

Jokes

Two friends are going up in the cable car ski lift. One has never been before.

"Hey," she says, "this thing looks dangerous. Big heavy car attached to that skinny little wire. Suppose it breaks?"

"It won't break."

"Wise guy, it won't break! What if it does."

"Look, I've been on this thing a million times. Anyway, that's not a wire, it's a thick cable. There's an auxiliary cable, so the first cable breaks – except it never breaks, but *if* it breaks, automatically the car is caught by the auxiliary cable."

"What if the electricity fails?"

"It never fails."

"Oh sure, it never fails. There couldn't be a first time? The current fails, look at the angle, we go sliding backward, we get hit against the mountain and goodbye Cholly."

"Look, you can't see it from here but they got an emergency brake. Anything goes wrong, the emergency brake goes on right away, automatically. So stop worrying."

"And if the brake don't take hold?"

"They've thought of that. Behind the first emergency brake they got a *second* one which takes over in a second".

"So what if they both fail?"

The friend gets desperate.

"On top of this car, you can't see, but they got two steel claws. In case both emergency brakes don't work, this is already impossible, but just in case, the two steel claws come together and grip tight the cable, the car is held in position until a rescue car comes up. You're in no danger whatsoever."

"And if the claws don't grip?"

The friend says, "Oh, you can kiss my ass."

A stranger says, "She could've kissed *mine* at the second emergency brake."

A senator visiting Africa from Washington DC addresses a large audience in the fields.

"Greetings from the President" Crowd: "Ubangwale".

"He has your interests in his mind" Crowd: "Ubangwale".

This goes on throughout the speech. On leaving he is told on the way to his car: "Please be careful not to step in the *Ubangwale*.

Jokes

A cannibal goes to the missionary who is in the pot. "Would you mind telling me how you spell your name. We are making out the menu."

Father goes to meet his daughter who is coming from Nairobi. She appears with a man that has an arrow through his nose, dressed with a tiger skin, a spear and a shield.
"Daddy, I want you to meet my new husband."
Her father says: "Honey, you never listen to me. I told you I wanted you to marry a *rich* doctor".

Man phones and the baby answers the phone.
"Can I speak to your daddy."
"No, he's busy."
"Can I then speak to your mummy".
"No, she's busy."
"Can I speak to someone."
"No they are all busy".
"What are they all doing?"
"They're looking for *me*!"

Husband packing his bags tells his wife he is going to Antigua as he has heard that there is a shortage of men and so they get £100 every time they make love. The wife starts packing too. He asks: "Where are you going?" She replies. "To Antigua. I want to see how you live on a hundred pounds a month".

Jokes

A man at the beach is sunbathing when a woman starts a conversation.
"Why are you so pale?"
"Because I'm just out of prison".
"What did you do?"
"I was serving 15 years for killing my wife".
"Oh, *so you're single!*"

A man is sitting in the living room and his wife says:
"Sidney, close the window. It's cold outside."
No answer. He goes on reading.
"Sidney, this is the third time I've asked you. Would you *please* close the window – it's *cold* outside."
He slams the window shut and says: "So now it's *warm* outside?"

Journalists often meet for lunch and tell stories. No one ever really listens, each one waiting for the moment where he can jump in with *his* gag. One day a journalist comes in, a bit later than the others, and says: "I don't look forward to going home. My mother is dying and the whole family is coming to stay." To which, a colleague replies: "If you think *that's* funny, listen to *this*!"

"Sam was a very generous man. He left £3,000 for the coffin, another £3,000 for the rabbi.
And £15,000 for the stone – LIKE IT?"

A man born with a humpback saves enough money to have an operation to correct his condition. When seeing the surgeon who will perform the operation, the surgeon looks at him: "You must have suffered a lot all these years as your face is wrinkled more than it should for your young years. For the same price, when you are under the anaesthetic, I will also give you a facelift."

The man is ready to leave hospital. He looks at himself in the mirror and indeed he looks like a new person. He goes out of the hospital, crosses the road and is killed by a car.

Now he is in Heaven and asks to see God.

"God," he tells Him, "I don't understand it. I have suffered all my life. I prayed for help. And now that I could have been happy You allowed me to die."

God replies: "My dear man. I was looking after you. But to tell you the truth, I didn't recognise you."

Mike Todd arrives in Heaven. St. Peter says:

"Mike, baby, are we glad you're here! We're all set to put on a great show – Mike, baby, when you see the script you'll flip! – and we've just been waiting for you!"

Todd says, "Wait a minute, what's all the rush? I haven't even got my coat off yet.  Whaddya mean, you're waiting for *me*? You got some great guys up here – Ziegfeld, De Mille..."

"Yeah, yeah, sure, they're here all right and they're great like you say. But Mike, baby, we need a guy who thinks *big*, know what I mean?"

"Well, okay, I don't want to let you guys down, but let's get one thing straight. I have complete authority – nobody, but *nobody*, tells me what to do. You dig?"

"Crazy! – you're in charge."

So Mike goes to work. He rehearses an aerial ballet with three hundred angels doing triple loops. He has Gabriel doing three solo choruses. After about three weeks rehearsal St. Peter comes around.

"Mike," he says, "look, I don't want you to get the idea I'm reneging on anything. I promised you complete autonomy and kept my word. It's just that – well – the Boss was wondering, have you got a part in the show for his son?"

A woman goes to a spiritualist because she wants to get in touch with the spirit of her husband. The medium goes into a trance and after a while a voice comes out.

"Jonquil," it says, "are you there?"

"That's Benny," the wife says, "I recognise his voice. Benny – tell me – are you all right?"

"Jonquil, I'm fine. It's gorgeous here. The sky is blue with a few nimbus clouds – my favourite type clouds. And the cows. Jonquil, I wish you could see those cows. Brown cows, white cows, black and white cows – such beautiful cows. I've never seen such beauty."

"Benny – I didn't know they had cows in heaven."

"Who's talking about *heaven*! I'm a *bull* in Argentina!"

The violinist Heifetz, does a recital tour through Sweden and has in his programme the Bach Chaconne. Realising that there are mainly farmers in the audience he decides that the Chaconne would be wasted on them and he plays something lighter. After the concert a farmer comes to the dressing room and says:

"I travelled fifty kilometres on my horse to hear you, and you didn't play the Chaconne."

Heifetz says, "My dear man, I had no idea that anyone here would either know or give a damn whether I played the Chaconne or not. Come back to my hotel, we'll have dinner and afterward I shall give you a private concert."

They go back and after dinner, a liqueur and a good cigar, Heifetz gets up, takes out his Amati violin and plays the Chaconne. When he finishes, the farmer says:

"Well, well, well. So that's the Chaconne. You know, Mr. Heifetz, that's the first time I ever heard it. I don't like it."

A man buys a canary that is singing beautifully. When the shopkeeper hands him the cage the man says, "Look, that sparrow in the cage with the canary – take him out, will you?"

The store keeper says, "The sparrow goes with the canary. I'm not charging you anything extra. If you want the canary, you have to *take* the sparrow."

"But this is ridiculous! The canary sings great, I want the canary, so why, for Christ's sake, do I have to *take* the sparrow?"

"The sparrow's his arranger."

The London Symphony is having a rehearsal. During a coffee break a man comes in and introduces himself to the orchestra manager.

"Mr. McDonald," he says, "I'd like to audition for you. I happen to be a first class player on every single instrument in the orchestra".

McDonald says, "I'm sure you're all you say you are but there are no vacancies. There is a long waiting list of musicians who want to get into this orchestra."

"Will you give me a chance and just listen!" the man yells. He grabs a viola and goes through the cadenza of the Walton Concerto. Picks up a violin and whips into Paganini's Twenty-fourth – Caprice. Rushes to the piano and plays Chopin's 5th. The musicians applaud and some even say, "Bravo!"

"Why do you do this?" says McDonald. "You're wasting your time and mine. It's not a question of your talent, there simply is no room..."

"For God's sake, just *wait* a minute and *listen*!" He leaps to a double-bass and goes into the rapid finale of Tchaikovsky's Fourth Symphony.

"Dammit," McDonald shouts, "how many times do I have to say it? I don't *care* how well you play, it doesn't *matter* how well you play, I'm trying to tell you there is *no* place for you in the orchestra at *all*!"

The man, absolutely exhausted, says, "Well I'll be a dirty sonofabitch!"

McDonald says, "Hey, that's different, we can always use a *conductor*!"

A famous violinist is at his hotel room in Nairobi after a most successful concert when he hears a scratching at his window. He opens it and there's a lioness.

"I do hope you'll excuse me," the lioness says. "We jungle folk are simply *dying* to hear your *wonderful* music. We couldn't possibly meet your fee but we've heard ever so much about your generosity – and we were just *hoping* and *praying* that you'll come and play for us. Could you *possibly...*"

"Sure," the violinist says, "what the hell. Wait, I'll get my fiddle."

So now in the jungle magic is being done. The minute the man starts to play a snake starts rubbing noses with a mongoose, a coyote and a deer snuggle close together, a tiger starts to nuzzle a cow. Suddenly a panther leaps out of a tree, jumps on the violinist, eats him up, eats the violin, eats the bow, everything.

The lioness goes up to the panther.

"What did you want to do that for? This man was just giving us a concert – for *free*, too – and you have to do such a thing. This *beautiful* music and you have to go and *ruin* it. *Why?*"

The panther (cupping a hand to his ear) asks, "What's that you say? Can't hear a word!"

A woman wakes up in the middle of the night and sees a man wearing an opera cloak. He starts toward her and she can see that instead of teeth he has fangs. Well, she's read her *Dracula* and she knows that a crucifix is one sure protection against vampires. She has a crucifix right by her; she grabs it and thrusts it out at him. He keeps coming towards her. She jumps to the foot of the bed and holds the crucifix right in front of his face. He says:

"Honeybunch, it vouldn't do you a *bit* of good."

A young man is talking to his mother.

"Mumsie," he says, "I want to have a long talk with you. You've probably noticed that my friendship for Marvin has become – how shall I say – well, it's ripened into something rich and sincere and true and good. Well, Mumsie, I love Marvin and Marvin loves me. We wish to announce our engagement and that's what this talk is about."

"Son," the mother says, "do you realise what you're saying?"

"Oh indeed, Mumsie, indeed I do. That's just why I've come to you; we've always been chums, you and I. I wouldn't dream of making a move without your blessing."

"But son – think what people will say – you cannot go against convention..."

"Oh, Mumsie, I can feel it coming on. I never would have thought it of you, Mumsie, of all people. Very well, let's have it out. What possibly objection could anyone have to my marrying Marvin?"

"He's Jewish!"

Jokes Jewish

A Jewish marriage broker arranges with a family to bring over a girl that he thinks is a fine match for their son. After the girl leaves, the family are furious:

"What kind of girl you're bringing here? A monster! One eye in the middle of her forehead, the left ear way up here, the right ear way down there, and the chin goes way back here…"

"Look here. You either *like* Picasso or you don't."

An old Jew is dying. His wife sits by his bedside and there is a terrible storm outside. A huge streak of lightning followed by a terrific clap of thunder. The old man sits up and says:

"I'm about to die. Send for a priest."

"Sam," his wife says, "you're losing your mind. Surely you mean a rabbi?"

"A rabbi should go out on a night like this?"

A girl from the Lower East Side in New York marries a Gentile who lives on Park Avenue. After her marriage she takes Momma to live with her and Momma speaks nothing but Yiddish. Daughter gets a tutor to teach Momma to speak English and after a year, daughter thinks Momma is ready to attend dinner parties. So at her next party, there is Momma sitting at the table, looking very elegant in a black Valentino but for a long time saying nothing at all. Suddenly Momma turns to the man at her right and begins talking to him in Yiddish. The daughter is mortified and she taps on the table to try to get Momma's attention:

"Mumsie darling, remember what you promised? Nothing but English, remember?"

The old lady nods, turns again to the man on her right and with great clarity says:

"You a no-good Fascist anti-Semite bastard. Did I say it right?"

Jokes Jewish

A man goes to his Rabbi and asks him where can he get a Honda for his son who wants it as a gift for his Bar mitzvah. The rabbi replies he does not know but to go and ask the rabbi around the corner who is young and knows all modern things.

He goes to see the young rabbi who explains to him that Honda is a motorcycle and suggests where he can go to get one. When he is about to leave, the rabbi asks: "Excuse me. What is a Bar mitzvah?"

Jewish mother takes her son to the Rijksmuseum in Amsterdam and shows him a painting of the Nativity.

"My son I want you to remember this as an example of Gentile mentality.

Money for a *hotel room* she hasn't got but she can have her *portrait* painted!"

Two men are compiling a Yiddish-English dictionary. They're on the "D's" and arrive at the word "disappointed." Neither of them can think of the Yiddish for it.

"Look," says one of them, "I'll call my mother. She only speaks Yiddish."

So he phones his mother and says to her, in Yiddish, "Momma, I can't come to dinner this Friday."

"Aiee, Boitrem, ah *zay* disappointed!"

A lady visits her doctor who tells her she is pregnant.
"But doctor, I'm sixty-five. And my husband, Sam, is ninety-two".
She leaves the office and phones her husband.
"You no good son-of-a-bitch, do you know what you've gone and done? You've got me pregnant!"
There's a long pause, then he says,
"Who is this?"

A tourist is walking with his wife in Paris. They find a perfume shop, the wife goes in and he waits outside. A streetwalker comes along and says to him, in English:
"Like to come home with me, cheri?"
"For how much?" says the tourist.
"Five thousand francs."
"I'll give you five hundred."
The girl spits at him and says "Je vous dis 'merde'" and walks away. A little later the man's wife comes out of the shop and they continue their walk. On the first corner they walk pass the same streetwalker. She takes one look at the man's wife and says to him:
"You see what you get for five hundred francs?"

A man goes to see his doctor.

"Doc," he says, "I got a funny kind of problem. When the wife and me was first married, it was really great, know what I mean? But lately, I dunno, it kinda lacks something. The whole thing's kinda, well, *boring*. No excitement, none of the old *uh-voom*!"

The doctor says, "How long have you been married?"

"Be thirty years next month".

"Well, you know," the doctor says, "you can't expect that honeymoon rapture to last forever. Thirty years, after all, that's a long time. You've said yourself that sex has become sort of routine with you. Maybe you even have a fixed schedule?"

"Well, yeah, Doc, now that you mention it – every second Friday, ten o'clock in the evening."

"Well then, why don't you try surprise? I mean, don't wait for the second Friday. Why not just when the impulse hits you? Right then and there."

"Sure, Doc, anything you say. And I'll letcha know how it works out."

He comes back the next day.

"Well, Doc, I took your advice. In fact, I was thinking about it all the way home. I thought to myself, that Doc's a shrewd cookie, he really knows. The more I thought of it, the better it sounded and started to get all worked up. And I figured, it's Thursday, she won't be expecting anything unusual and – well, by that time I was home. I rang the bell, I didn't have my key and my wife opened the door. I came in and the hall – well, the dining room's just off the hall, see? So before my wife can figure out what's happening, I just grabbed her and pushed her into the dining room, right onto the table and boy, it was great! And the whole time I'm thinking to myself, that Doc's a killer, he's really on the ball. But then, after a while, I dunno, the whole thing got kinda boring – none of that old *uh-voom*, know what I mean? But I'll say one thing – it made a *hell* of a hit with our dinner guests."

An American and a Chinese are having lunch and the American tells his friend how much he admires the oriental way of life. The Chinese agrees and he tells him: "We do things differently. For instance you are always in a rush for everything. We instead take things calmly. When I make love to my wife I start by caressing her. I stop. We sip warm sake. I caress her again. I stop. I read to her passages from Keats and Lovelace. I caress her again. And then, and only then I proceed to the act of making love."

That night in bed with his wife he begins to caress her, which he hasn't done in thirty years. He stops. Brings her a beer and they sip the beer. He caresses her again. He stops. He reads her the Editorial of the *Jewish Chronicle*. He stops. He's about to caress her again when she asks him: "Sam, what has come over you? You are making love like a Chinaman."

"Mama what's a Lesbian?"
"What do you mean, what's a Lesbian, indeed! What a question! You just wait till your step-father gets home. Ask her!"

A man tells his wife that the doctor has told him that he is likely to die in the night and asks her to make love to him as it will be his last night. She acceeds. A couple of hours later he asks her again. She goes along with his request. Two hours later when he asks her again, she replies "It's OK for you – you don't have to get up in the morning!"

Jokes

A doctor prescribes a new potency drug for his patient and suggests he takes one to see his reaction.

A few days later he visits his doctor with the news that the drug he gave him is 'absolutely disgraceful'. "Well, I must admit that it's partially my fault. I didn't take it until last night and instead of one I took four. I went on the rampage and practically raped my wife. I leaped up and dragged her onto the table – oh, it was awful. Broke all the dishes, knocked over a bottle of wine, ruined the tablecloth. I've never behaved like that in my entire life!"

"This is dreadful," the doctor says, "and even though you did disregard my instructions, I still feel partially to blame. Can I pay for the damages?"

"Don't you give it a thought, Doctor – I'm quite sure they'll never let us in *that* restaurant again."

A man returns home and finds his best friend with his wife in bed.
He looks at them and addresses his friend: "I have to, but you?

A man goes to a brothel. He says to the madam:
"I'm a perverted fellow. I like to beat women and I have my own
whip. Can you do anything for a terrible person like me?"
The madam says, "Oh, sure, we get all types, but beating, that
comes pretty high. You'll have to give the girl a hundred pounds."
He accepts, picks out a girl and they go upstairs. He gives her a
hundred pounds and then begins to beat her. After a while she
says:
"Hey, how long does this go on?"
He says, "Till you give back the hundred pounds."

A man comes for his first visit to a psychiatrist. He
seems deeply depressed, doesn't react much to anything.
The psychiatrist decides to test him to see if he has any
of the more obvious fetishes. He shows him a collection
of shoes followed by whips, chains, knives. No reaction.
The psychiatrist then opens a closet full of women's
evening dresses.
    The patient's eyes light up and he reaches out for one.
The psychiatrist slaps his hand.
    "Don't you *dare* touch that one – it's *mine*!"

A woman goes to see the doctor. The doctor asks her what's wrong.
"Nothing much, really," the woman says, "just that I'm dead."
"Dead, eh? Did you know that dead people don't bleed?"
"No. That's new to me."
Suddenly the doctor jabs the woman's thumb with a pin. A drop of blood appears.
"Well, how about that!", the woman says. "Dead people *do* bleed!"

A woman goes to see a psychiatrist. "I have this illusion," she says. "I don't have it all the time, but every once awhile I get this very strong feeling that I'm a dog."

The psychiatrist says, "Well, whatever it is, we'd better investigate. Would you please lie down on the couch?"

The woman says, "Oh no, I'm not allowed on the couch."

Doctor to patient: "Would you strip, please. That's the ugliest body I've even seen."
Patient: "That's what my G.P. says."
Doctor: "Then, why did you come to see me?"
Patient: "I wanted a second opinion."

A man goes to see a psychiatrist who asks him the reason for the visit.

"Well," the man says, "it's my friends, really. They're worried about this screw I have in my navel. It doesn't bother me at all but it does bother my friends so, just to please them, I made an appointment to see you."

After forty minutes of conversation the psychiatrist says:

"Do you have confidence in me?"

"Well," the man says, "I must say you're different from what I expected."

"I see. Then, I want you to do something for me. When you go to bed tonight, have a screwdriver handy; take the screwdriver and just take the screw *out* of your navel. Then, come in tomorrow at eleven".

Next morning at eleven there he is. The psychiatrist greets him and says, "Did you do as I suggested?"

"Of course," the man says, "I *said* I would, and I *did*."

"You took the screw out of your navel?"

"Yes."

"So what happened?"

"So what happened! My ass fell off!"

Jokes Golf

At the first hole on a gold course a man tees off, hits a hard drive but the ball hooks badly and goes off the course entirely. The man figures it's a lost ball, puts another ball down and starts again. He plays nine holes when a policeman comes up to him:

"Sir, did you lose a ball awhile back?"

"Yes, I did. Why?"

"Well, sir, I'm afraid I've got bad news for you. Your ball struck a cyclist, causing him to swerve right into the path of an oncoming bus. The bus hit a wall and we don't know yet how many are injured."

The man says, "But this is dreadful – I had no idea – is there anything I can do?"

"Well sir, next time you could open the face of your club a little, like this..."

God and Moses are playing golf. Moses tees off, hits a beautiful drive that lands on the green, just a few feet away from the hole. God takes a few practice swings, tees off, tops the ball badly, it rolls along the ground. A groundhog sees the rolling ball, picks it up in his teeth and moves off. An eagle swoops on the groundhog, picks it up and, as the eagle is flying over the first hole, lightning strikes the eagle, it lets go of the  groundhog which falls onto the green, the ball drops out of the groundhog's mouth, it rolls into the cup, a hole in one.

Moses says, "All right, all right. You wanna play golf or do you just wanna fuck about?"

Two men are playing behind two women who are going very slowly. One says to the other: "Go and ask them if we can go in front of them".

One goes and returns quickly and tells his friend: "I can't. One is my wife and the other is my mistress."

"Don't worry. I'll go."

He comes back rather quickly: *"Small world!"*

A rabbi is on his way to synagogue on Yom Kippur, the Day of Atonement. He passes his golf club on the way and feels that as it's very early in the morning and no one is around, it's quite safe to play a few holes. He goes to the locker room, gets his clubs, tees up a ball and starts taking a few practice swings. At this point Moses, who has been watching the whole thing from Heaven, calls to God:

"Hey, Boss, look what's happening – you won't believe it. Here it is Yom Kippur and guess who's going to play golf – a rabbi!"

God says, "I know all about it. Who do you think you're talking to anyway? I not only know but don't you worry – I'm going to punish him."

The rabbi hits a beautiful drive, straight down the fairway, the ball lands on the green, drops into the cup, a hole in one.

Moses says, "Hey, what goes on here. A rabbi plays golf on Yom Kippur, you say you're going to punish him, and he makes a hole in *one*!"

God says, "So, who can he tell?"

Some kids are playing marbles in a vacant lot.
Some pigeons alight and are in the kids' way.
The kids say:
　"Fuck off, fuck off".
　A priest just passing at that moment hears
this. He comes over to the kids.
　"Now children," he says. "that is no way to talk
to the little birdies. Do you wish them to go away?
Then you must say, 'Shoo, Shoo.' *Then* they
will fuck off."

A man goes to a confessional booth.
　"Father, my name is Sid Abramowitz.
I'm 87 years old. Last night, at a bar, I
picked up a girl, we went back to her flat
and we made love like in my *life* I've never
made love."
　The priest says, "Just a moment. Aren't
you a Jew?"
　"Yes that's right."
　"Then shouldn't you be talking to a
rabbi? Why are you telling me?"
　"I'm telling *everybody*".

A friend asks his companion. "Do you think that history would have been different had Khrushchev been assassinated instead of Kennedy?"

"I don't know," his friend replies. "But I am quite sure Onassis wouldn't have married Mrs. Khrushchev."

During Watergate, Nixon's press adviser says he has a great idea.

"We're going to get you circumcised, that will get all the Jews behind you, you really need them, it will make headlines."

So they send for the man who performs the operation. He's in the bedroom three hours with Nixon, finally comes out, exhausted. "It's impossible," he says, "I can't do it. There's no end to this prick!"

Bill Clinton dies and goes to Heaven. St. Peter greets him: "Bill you just made it to Heaven. Welcome. But you are going to have to prove that you deserve being here. You have to do penance."

Clinton: "I'll do *anything*."

"You see Stalin making love to Marilyn Monroe? Well you have to make love to Golda Meier who is waiting right there."

Clinton: "But that is not fair. Stalin is doing penance too and he is making love to Marilyn Monroe and I have to make love to Golda Meir!"

"You have it wrong", says St. Peter. "It is *Marilyn Monroe* who is doing penance, not Stalin."

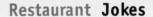

Garçon, il y a
un mouche dans
ma soupe.

UNE mouche!

"Won Ton soup, Moo goo gai pan and
flied lice."
"You *know* it's fried rice, you can pronounce fried rice. So why don't you *say*
fried rice. Ya PLICK!"

A very rich American takes a cruise in the QE 2. He is of course asked to sit at
the Captain's table and for two days just before lunch and dinner all the guests
say '*Bon Appetit*' to which he replies '*Goldberg*'. He is puzzled by this and
decides to tell the story to the PR purser and seek an explanation.

"Mr. Goldberg," the purser says "when the guests say *bon appetit* they are
wishing you an enjoyable meal."

Mr. Goldberg feels bad about this and decides to be the first to speak that
evening. He raises his glass and says: '*Bon appetit*'. And everyone replied:
'*Goldberg*'.

Have I ever told you...

Two friends dining at an
expensive restaurant:
"The food here is absolutely awful."
"Yes – and such small portions."

Customer asks for 'a lousy breakfast.'
Waiter replies: "We don't serve lousy breakfasts."
"And why not? You served me one yesterday."

The *best* restaurant is where they know you.

Customer to waiter: "I would like a table near a waiter, please."

A waiter turns to the customer who has left him a one pound tip on a thirty pound bill, returns the pound and says: "Here. You need it more than me!"

Dining with a friend when I was a restaurant critic:
"Larry, I simply get the impression, when I read your
articles, that if *you* enjoy a restaurant, so will I."

She: "Would you love me if I were a transvestite?"

He: "I don't know.
Let's get a Vest first and see."

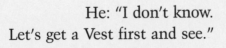

Jokes

A vasectomy means never having to say you are sorry.

"God. Only You can help me in my terrible predicament. My only son is about to turn Christian!"
"Your son!"

At a restaurant one friend says to the other: "That's Robert de Niro."
"Wasn't he 'Raging Bull'?"
"I think so – why don't you go and ask him."
The friend approaches Mr. de Niro's table and asks him:
"Are you Robert de Niro?"
He says: "Yes, I am"
"Are you 'Raging Bull'?"
"MOO!"

A couple go to see their doctor to discuss the behaviour of their children. One boy seems very positive and the other extremely pessimistic. The doctor suggest that as Christmas is coming to get a bag of manure for the positive boy and an electric train for the pessimist.

The boys are opening their Christmas gifts when the pessimistic boy cries: "An electric train. My parents want to electrocute me."

The positive boy when seeing the bag of manure exclaims with joy: "There must be a pony around!"

A man is in a terrible car accident lying on the side of the road with passers-by surrounding him and hears one say: "My God, he's in a dreadful way, he's lost his left arm!" At which the injured man cries: "My Rolex, my Rolex is gone!"

Two friends talking:
"Were you upset by the stock market crash?"
"No. Last night I slept like a baby. I woke up every hour and cried."

Jokes

Mrs. Thatcher on one of her visits to Russia is at lunch with President Gorbachev. He tells her:

"To honour your visit, please ask me anything you would like."

Mrs. Thatcher replies: "I would like you to open the borders for twenty-four hours and anyone who wants to leave, can."

Gorbachev looks at her and says: "Margaret, baby – you little devil. You want to be left alone with me."

A man calls a plumber. After half an hour
the plumber tells him:
"It's fixed. You owe me a hundred pounds."
The man looks at the plumber in astonish-
ment, "That's outrageous. A hundred
pounds for half an hour's work. I don't
make that as a stockbroker".
"Neither could I when I was a stockbroker."

A man wakes up in hospital with both arms and legs in plaster. He asks his friend:

"What happened?"

"You climbed out on the window ledge. Said you would take off, then fly back."

"Why didn't you stop me?"

"Stop you? I was *betting* on you!"

Mixed emotions are what you feel when your mother-in-law drives off a cliff in your new Cadillac.

"Don't you ever clean your fucking chimney?"

Have I ever told you...

Puns

"Noah, I want you to build another Ark."

"Right Lord."

"How many decks on the first one?"

"Two Lord."

"Make it bigger – like ten. And instead of animals, let's have fish."

"Okay Lord."

"Not any old fish – CARP."

"Gotcha, Lord. You want me to build You a Multi-Storey Carp-Ark!"

Puns and plays on words

Going to the opening of a Thai Restaurant, the restaurant critic stops to say to his companion: "I hope they will let me in without a thai."

I wonder if Monica Lewinsky had been Harmonica Lewinsky if it would have been better for me.

I have always wanted to order fish in a restaurant and have it a long time in coming so I can say to the waiter: Long time no sea bass.

A lady pianist named Hatch
Who was expert in Mozart and Bach
But said if you are fussy
For Brahms or Debussy
Siddown and I'll playez a snatch

De Gaulle visiting England. Mme De Gaulle is asked what would she like most: She replies: "I wish for a penis."
De Gaulle tells her, "My dear, I believe the British pronounce it happiness".

The Lord Mayor of London, wearing his robes of office, is entertaining the Queen of Norway. She's wearing a low-cut gown and in the cleft of her bosom she wears a rose.
He asks: "Would you blush if I plucked your rose?"
And she replies: "Would you flush if I pulled your chain?"

Reading a review in a newspaper after one of my performances I was amused to learn that I was a "living leg-end".

I would like to play it with them live (what a silly word; could I play it any other way?)

Are you rushin'?
No, I'm Jewish.

Puns and plays on words

A man sees a dog drowning in a pond. He jumps in and gives mouth-to-mouth resuscitation.

A passer by stops and asks him: "Are you a vet?"

To which he replies: "Am I vet. I'm soaked!".

During Christmas on one of my visits to perform for the inmates in jail I stood waiting to get their attention to start my show. When that happened, I looked at them and said: "Now that I have a captive audience"... and started playing to great applause.

"You're like Napoleon. I love your boney parts."

A teacher asks one of her young students: "John, what did you do yesterday?"

"Miss, I road on the choo choo".

"Oh no," the teacher replies. "From today, we are all going to use adult words and stop using baby talk. It is not choo choo – it is train. Now, Peter, what did you do?"

"My daddy and I watched TV."

"No, Peter. It is not your daddy. Your father watched TV with you. Larry, what did you do last night?"

"I read a children's book."

"What's the name of the book?"

"Oh, miss. Just a children's book."

"Larry, tell me the name of the book," the teacher insists.

"Winnie, the shit".

"Here's the sick squid I owe you!"

Puns and plays on words

The Pope lands at Kennedy Airport in New York. When the journalists ask what does he think of the brothels in New York, the Pope cleverly responds: "Are there any brothels in New York?" The headlines the following morning: Pope's first words on landing in New York: "Are there any brothels in New York?"

"Do you accept Luncheon Vultures?"

Anecdotes

Anecdotes

I was asked to write the score for a film called *Genevieve* – a comedy about the Veteran Car Club annual London to Brighton run. The line that decided me that I *had* to do *Genevieve* was when Dinah Sheridan, married (in the film) to John Gregson, asks him: "Alan… proper lunch or proper dinner?"

They didn't have the money to pay my fee – they offered me a two-and-a-half percent of the producer's share. My agent strongly advised me against it but I loved the film, wanted to do it and I accepted that I might end up with the price of a hamburger. In fact within a month of release, *Genevieve* was making a profit. The four leads got £1500 each, a flat fee, with no participation in the proceeds. I was making far more out of the film than the stars; in fact my children went to college on *Genevieve*. The score was nominated for an Oscar.

Ingrid Bergman recorded Lincoln's Gettysburg Address, which I accompanied on the mouth organ. I still use it during my one-man shows. I always thought that had Ingrid instead of Lincoln read the Address, the South would have won.

Groucho Marx and I were together in a lift. A Catholic priest turns to Groucho and says to him "My mother adores you." Groucho replies "I didn't know you fellows were *allowed* to have mothers".

During the war, but before the US entered, I couldn't get mouth organs. They were made by M. Hohner in Germany and the supply, not surprisingly, was cut off. When I met the Minister of Supply in Churchill's government, I asked him if he knew how I could get hold of some German mouth organs. No, he said, he didn't know, 'but if you find a way, do tell us so we can put a stop to it.'

They were more accommodating in Czechoslovakia. I made a little joke in my show saying I'd be grateful if some GI could 'liberate' a few mouth organs for me. A sackful, all Larry Adler models, were delivered 'with the compliments of the Czech army.'

I was one of the first performers to go to Israel to entertain the troops. I was met at the airport by Major Zafrir, from Army Special Services, who told me about a song, 'Sharm-el-Sheikh', that had become very popular in the Army. It had been written *during* the battle for Sharm-el-Sheikh by an Israeli soldier, Rafi Gabai. Not only that but, standing at his left, apparently, there was a publisher because there was already a record out and it was a hit. I learned the song, a very good one, and my first chance to play it was at the former Egyptian airbase, El Arish, in the Sinai. There were about 2000 soldiers. I stood on a tank and played 'Sharm-el-Sheikh'. The reception was tremendous, so much so that I had to play it again. In fact they made me play it six times. Then I raised my hand for quiet.

"My friends, I am deeply moved by your reception of what is, after all, *your* song. But there are other artists waiting and I don't want to hold up the show. So please, don't ask me to play it again."

And an Israeli soldier calls out, "You'll play it till you get it *right*!"

Anecdotes

In 1943 I went to Africa with Jack Benny and other artists to do shows at military bases. When the USO tour was announced, Marshall Field, who had founded the Chicago *Sun*, suggested that I do weekly dispatches for the *Sun*. The idea delighted me. I'd always wanted to write. It was agreed that my fees would go to the Red Cross. Having accepted I became nervous about it – having not written one before.

I asked Samuel Grafton, the political columnist for the New York *Post*, how did one write a dispatch. "Simple", he said. "You write down what happens each day, then you write at the top, 'This is a Dispatch' and that's it."

I bought a light Hermes typewriter at Macy's, which, as I had seen photos of Ernie Pyle with a similar machine, made me feel a real war correspondent.

The committee thought that the articles were so well written that I must have found a ghost-writer. After all, I was a mouth organist. I wrote daily dispatches and each piece had to be submitted to Army censorship. Sometimes so many lines were scissored out the page looked like a lace curtain. The censors didn't say I had written lies; they just cut out the truth.

I once wrote one of Jack Benny's shows. We worked well together but as much as I respected him I did not want to be another of his writers. Jack however told everyone from his own writers to George Burns that I was the world's funniest man. This annoyed the writers, especially since Jack, at a script conference, would say that he wished Larry Adler was there as *he* would know how to make that joke work.

It had all started when we were both invited by the Sultan of Morocco in Marrakech. We had to go through two huge iron gates, each looking as if they weighed several tons, drawn back by guards. As we went in, I whispered: "Mind your manners, Jack, don't slam the door."

Returning from a very late engagement in Brighton I left the theatre and noticed that the road which I remembered as a two way had become a No Entry. I decided to follow the route I knew anyway and mid-way down the street I was stopped by a policeman, who asked me: "Didn't you see the No Entry sign?"

I replied. "Yes I saw it."

"Then why did you drive in?"

"In the hope I wouldn't find *you*."

On a very narrow street my front bumper touched the side of a lorry driving on the opposite side. The driver stopped and, furious, approached me. I put my hand out and said: "Stop. I bet you that you won't be able to say anything to me without using the words 'fuck you'!" To which he laughed – we both laughed – and exchanged insurance details.

Al Capone told me this story: One of his men had killed a man in broad daylight. It looked as if he would get a first degree murder conviction which carried the death penalty. "So", said Capone, "I had to get to a bribable juror. Paid him $25,000 to hold out for manslaughter, which carried a two to twenty-year prison sentence. The jury brought in a verdict of manslaughter. I gave a banquet for the juror which cost me another 25 G's and said to him: "How did you do it? I never thought you'd get away with manslaughter."

"Oh boy", said the Juror, "you don't know how difficult it was. They wanted to *acquit* him!"

Anecdotes

Charlie Chaplin's son and mine were found taking coins from one of the fountains at Westminster. They appeared at the Magistrates Court charged with stealing money from the Council. The Judge found them 'not guilty' with the words "I do not understand why Westminster Council chooses to keep their money in a fountain instead of the Bank".

One day the jazz saxophonist, Frankie Trumbauer, took me inside Paul Whiteman's dressing room and asked him to listen me play. I played *When Day is Done*, my interpretation cribbed from his own record of the piece. Whiteman then asked me to play *Rhapsody in Blue*. The piece was much too complex for me at that time but as I didn't want to admit this to Whiteman, I said: 'I don't like *Rhapsody in Blue*'. Whiteman turned to a young man I hadn't noticed before and asked him: 'What do you think of *that*, Gershwin; this kid doesn't LIKE *Rhapsody in Blue*. That's how I met Gershwin.

We became friends and on occasions we played *Rhapsody in Blue* together. George made a piano roll which I use nowadays in my one man shows. It is an eerie sensation as it is as if George were there in person. In fact some times I feel he plays better than others.

George and I dated the same girl, Simone Simon (pronounced See-moan, See-moan). Simone invited Gershwin and me to dinner, without telling either that the other was coming. George and I glared at each other across the table, wondering what sadistic joy Simone was getting out of this. We found out when two sound technicians arrived from Fox and set up a recording machine. Simone wanted George to play the piano, me, the mouth organ, while she sang arias from *Porgy and Bess*.

My first introduction to British sportsmanship: At a tennis competition I was baffled when my opponent would cry, 'Good shot!, well played!' When he won a point he would say, 'Sorry'. He accepted his victory with regret and implied that I was a spiffingly good sport to let him win when it was obvious that I could have walked away with the match.

It was my agent, Charles Cochran, who started the legend that I use a new mouth organ every time I play. He launched into an ad-lib to fill time during a radio broadcast. I couldn't contradict Cochran on the air and so I agreed with his statement before playing a number. Several thousand letters were received asking for my used mouth organs.

I once won a name-dropping contest with Walter Cronkite. His top story involved dining with Jackie and John Kennedy. Mine: Charles Chaplin phoned me to make a fourth at tennis – Bill Tilden had dropped out. I joined Chaplin at the tennis court where he was hitting against a lady with badly combed hair and a man with a weird moustache. After hitting for a while, the lady suggested that we start a set. The minute she spoke I realised it was Garbo. The man was Salvador Dali.

I was playing for the troops when heavy firing was heard. I stopped playing and said: "I didn't realise we were so near the firing line." And someone answered: "Those are music critics."

Anecdotes

When I was playing at the Alhambra in Paris I included Ravel's *Bolero* in my repertoire. I was surprised when I heard that Maurice Ravel had heard that I played his *Bolero* and wanted to hear me. Ravel opened the door, took the record and played it. Until then I had thought it was a good record, it was a big seller and I was proud of it. Standing there whilst its composer listened to it I was aware of imperfections and mistakes. When it finished Ravel asked why did I play it that fast and why had I made cuts. I explained that my act ran fifteen minutes, which was the length of *Bolero*. I loved the number but, to include it, I had to make cuts. Years later Ravel's publishers informed me that Ravel had left instructions that I was to have free rights to play *Bolero* in whatever medium I pleased. That right is unique to me.

During a cabaret performance, one man at a ringside table was being noisy. I never know how to cope with a drunk so I ignored him. During *Bolero* he hit the floor with a thud. I later found that he was rising and falling to the beat of *Bolero* and, on one rise, someone had pulled out his chair. Later in the foyer I saw the drunk. He turned out to be an old friend.

"Larry", he said, "have you been inside? There's a fellow doing your stuff, pinching your act – but he's *terrible*!"

Once I stayed at a hotel in St. Germain-en-Laye, and heard from the adjoining suite a burst of piano-playing. Simply magnificent. I asked at the front desk who was the pianist only to be told: 'Someone with a strange name – it is Or-row-weets." I told him that he was considered to be the world's greatest pianist. The clerk seemed uninterested and bored until I told him that he was married to Toscanini's daughter. And that's how Horowitz became a celebrity in St.Germain-en-Laye.

I was on the maiden voyage of the Queen Mary. Henry Hall and I were to broadcast *Rhapsody in Blue* in mid Atlantic to both the US and Europe. We got the green light and we were on. When the number was over we were informed that something had gone wrong and that we weren't on the air.

"When did you find out?" I asked.

"A few seconds after you started."

"Why didn't you stop us?"

"I *like Rhapsody in Blue*."

I had to do a number in *Many Happy Returns*, a film that starred Ray Milland. The director told me that I'd do the solo with Guy Lombardo's orchestra. I said I didn't like Lombardo's band. I liked Duke Ellington. He told me that no-one had asked me what I *liked* and that he was telling me what I was going to *do*. I refused and was fired.

The next day the producer sent for me. He tried to talk me into doing the number with Lombardo. He reminded me that I had a contract and that I was reneging on a signed agreement. He pointed out that whilst I was making $300, Duke Ellington would cost twenty thousand. Of course it didn't make sense. I still refused.

I was amazed when the next day I was told over the phone that they had got Ellington for me. Duke couldn't appear in the picture as Lombardo was one of the film's stars and I don't know if Lombardo ever knew about Ellington playing behind my solo.

Anecdotes

Ira Gershwin had given me as a birthday present the manuscript of *Lullaby Time*, a string quartet written by George Gershwin which had never been published or even performed.

Morton Gould had rescored *Lullaby Time* for mouth organ and strings and I first played this version with the Ulster Symphony at the Belfast Festival in 1967. In introducing the piece I told the story of how George's brother Ira had given me the piece and only a *schmuck* like me would stand up in Belfast and plug a name spelled I-R-A.

I appeared in the film St. Martin's Lane, which was being made by Charles Laughton's Company. Rex Harrison, David Burns and I tried to teach a number to Vivien Leigh. She was slow picking it up but finally Rex exclaimed, "I think she's got it!" Then we all did a celebration dance. I believe the 'Rain in Spain' sequence in *My Fair Lady* derived from that number but my only evidence is that Rex Harrison was in both.

In 1940 Dinah Shore and I provided the cabaret at the White House Correspondents' dinner to President Roosevelt. It was very well received. I came off, and a lady in the wings congratulated me and remarked that I seemed in great form.
"Thank you", I said, "your face is so familiar, but with the excitement I..."
She said, "Mrs. Roosevelt."

The mouth organ repertoire isn't huge but some great composers have written works for me. After hearing me, Dr. Ralph Vaughan Williams, wondered if he was right in thinking that I exhaled to produce C and inhaled to produce D – which would make it impossible to achieve a true legato. Logically, yes. However, I suggested, I would play a slow melody, the second movement of the Violin Concerto in A Minor by Bach. I would be changing the breath direction constantly. I did this and then asked Vaughan Williams if he could tell *when* my breath changed. The Grand Old Man of English Music admitted he couldn't tell when I was inhaling and when exhaling.

I was later told that Vaughan Williams had decided to write an original work for me. Despite my careful exposition of what a mouth organ could and could not do, his new piece had written chords and intervals that simply could not be played without using auxiliary lungs. I went to see him in Dorking and I explained, not without nervousness, that there were a few bits that needed redoing. To which he replied:

"Well, if you don't like it the way I wrote it' – he paused, timing it in a way that Jack Benny would have admired – "I'll change it. If you don't like it after that I'll change it once more. But if, after that, you *still* don't like it, I'm going to re-score the whole bloody thing for *bass tuba*!"

I was booked to play it at the Proms, at the Albert Hall, with Sir Malcolm Sargent conducting the London Symphony Orchestra attended by Vaughan Williams. The performance was one of the best I have ever given. The applause mounted in intensity. Sargent gestured to Vaughan Williams who stood up. The audience went into the kind of hysteria you associate with Sting and Elton John. Sargent tapped his baton, nodded to me and indicated that he would play the work a second time. *The Times* wrote that 'last night the Vaughan Williams received both its first and its second performance…'

Anecdotes

On tour I'd visit hospitals. One child had had his hands blown off by a grenade. I suggested to him that, if he held a mouth organ with his wrists, it could be held securely and he could learn to play it. He stared at me morosely and didn't seem to respond. Just before I left the hospital a nurse told me the kid had changed his mind and would I give him a lesson. I did. He became a taxi-driver, had a full licence, driving with his wrists.

Another was just lying on a bed. He was in shock. The nurse asked me to play for him but warned me that I wouldn't get any reaction – I would think he doesn't hear but they all thought he did. After a couple of numbers his lips moved. He asked for Beethoven. I said which Beethoven. He wanted *Ode to Joy*, the finale of the *Ninth Symphony*. Soldiers, some in wheelchairs, some on crutches, came into the room and sang it. The soldier sat up in his bed and *he* began to sing. That incident started his complete recovery. It is why I am very glad that I am a musician.

When someone told James Thurber that he had read a French translation of Thurber's *My Life and Hard Times* and that 'it read even better in French', Thurber replied: "Yes, I know. My work tends to lose something in the original."

I love tennis. I was very lucky to be invited to Wimbledon every year by one of the highest ranking officials. I later learned that he was a thwarted mouth organist and had nearly been a non-thwarted one. He had as a teenager auditioned for the Borrah Minevitch Harmonica Rascals who had accepted him. Since they did not accept me, he could reasonably claim that he was a better mouth organist than I was. It's the single greatest perk I've ever had.

After my last recital I was booked to fly Tel Aviv-New York. We flew El Al. The plane stopped to refuel at Heathrow Airport but developed engine trouble and it seemed we'd be sitting in the airport lounge overnight.

A BOAC man approached me and said that BOAC could put me on their flight leaving that night for New York. I said I appreciated the offer and would like to accept but, as I'd been sitting with an extremely nice lady with whom I'd chatted all the way from Tel Aviv to London, I wondered if it would be possible to accommodate her as well. He went to check and returned smiling. All was in order. He sneaked the lady and me out of the lounge, arranged for the transfer of our luggage from El Al to BOAC and that's how I gave a lift to Golda Meir.

At one of my performances, James Thurber asked me to play *The Tennessee Waltz* for him. I explained to the audience that, although I considered the tune too sentimental, I'd be happy to play it. When I finished playing, Thurber stood up.
"I first encountered the name of Larry Adler in print", he said, "and then I heard it said, and then I said it, and it seemed to me a common ordinary name like Abe Lincoln. And then I heard him play and the name was lighted as with the light of stars and I knew it would last as long as music, which is to say forever – and if that isn't sentimental, whatever was?"

At lunch the following day I told him that I would have given anything to have had a tape recorder. He told me that he would dictate it to me, word by word, as he had a phonographic memory. This is how I am able to reprint it.

Anecdotes

On meeting the husband of a showgirl I was escorting back from a party at 4 a.m. he remarks: 'This is a hell of a time to be running around the street with a man.' 'But darling' she replies, 'it's not a *man* – it's Larry!'

Before achieving notoriety I was often asked: "What is your name and what do you do?" I would of course reply, My name is Larry Adler and I play the mouth organ. Big pause. "Ah, but what do you *really* do?"

When Placido Domingo told me that he had mimicked to one of my tunes to learn the mouth organ for a film audition, I asked him. "Did you drop the mouth organ to become a singer?"

Biographical Notes

Biographical Notes

Larry Adler has been playing classical, jazz and popular music for seven decades. He is the only mouth organist listed in Who's Who, Grove's Dictionary and the Oxford Companion to Music.

Born in Baltimore on February 10, 1914, he studied piano at the Peabody Conservatory of Music and achieved a distinction that is still unique; he is the only student they ever expelled (for changing his recital piece from *Waltz in A Minor* by Grieg, to *Yes, we have no bananas*). Peabody forgave him; in 1985 they celebrated their 90th anniversary and invited Larry Adler as their guest of honour and awarded him an honorary diploma.

His film appearances include *Many Happy Returns* (Paramount), *The Singing Marine* (Warner Bros.), *Music for Millions* and *Three Daring Daughters* (MGM), *St.Martin's Lane* with Charles Laughton, Vivian Leigh and Rex Harrison (Mayflower Productions). He has composed film scores for *King & Country*, *High Wind in Jamaica*, *The Hook*, *The Great Chase* and best of all, *Genevieve* for which he received an Academy Award nomination.

Composers who have written works for him include Darius Milhaud, Arthur Benjamin, Malcolm Arnold, Francis Chagrin, Gordon Jacob, Joaquin Rodrigo and Ralph Vaughan Williams.

Larry Adler's recording of *Le Grisbi* won the *Grand Prix du Disque*.

He marked his 80th birthday by releasing a CD *The Glory of Gershwin*, produced by Sir George Martin which featured amongst others: Sting, Elton John, Cher and Sinead O'Connor – it's a bestseller around the world. It earned him a place in the Guinness Book of Records as the oldest artist to reach the British pop charts.

For eight years, in the US, he toured in joint recital with the dancer, Paul Draper. His one man show, *From Hand to Mouth*, has been featured at the Edinburgh, Dublin, Zurich and other festivals. Orchestras with which he has appeared as soloist include the BBC, LPO, Northern Sinfonia, Chicago Symphony (with Solti), the San Francisco (with Monteux), the Detroit (with Ormandy), Baltimore, North Carolina, Cleveland and the Los Angeles Philharmonic at the Hollywood Bowl. The Vaughan Williams Romance for Mouth organ, Piano and Strings was premiered at the Proms.

In 1949 he moved to London after becoming involved in the defence of those suspected of communist sympathies during the McCarthy witch-hunt in the United States. "Resist the pressure to conform," he advises young people. "Better be a lonely individualist than a contented conformist."

He appears on many radio and TV programmes in the UK and abroad. He ad libbed *Summertime* with Itzhak Perlman on the Parkinson show and this performance inspired Torvill & Dean to use Adler's recording of *Summertime* for the skating routine with which they won their first international award in Copenhagen.

Larry Adler's avocation is writing: besides his autobiography *It Ain't Necessarily So* (Collins), he has written *Jokes and How to Tell Them* (Doubleday) in the US; articles and columns on a wide range of subjects, usually infused with humour, for *Punch*, *What's On in London*, the *New Statesman*, *Spectator*, *Observer*, *Sunday Times*, the *New York Times*, *The Oldie* and others.

He loves conversation and enjoys telling stories during his musical engagements and TV appearances.

In 1988 Larry Adler was made a Fellow of Yale University. He has been married twice, has four children and two grandchildren.

Just as we went to press, Larry died
on the 6th of August 2001, in London.

In Memoriam Larry Adler 1914 - 2001

press extracts

"Larry Adler, the lengendary harmonica player. Always a witty companion."
Glenys Roberts, *Daily Mail*

"Harmonica King Adler was noted as a raconteur, composer and champion of liberal causes."
Mark Jagasia, *Daily Express*

"His is the voice that will not be stilled".
Illtyd Harrington, *Camden New Journal*

"He earned household-name status as much for his lively and humorous public personality as for his musicianship."
Richard Severo, *The New York Times*

"The noble sounds that Mr. Adler can persuade his mouth organ to give forth are quite beyond belief... he keeps his audience shuttling happily between admiration and amusement."
The Daily Telegraph

"Sophisticated and still witty, traditional in a sense and yet out-rageously funny, musically entertaining and verbally humorous, Larry Adler should not be missed..."
Evening Chronicle. Newscastle.

"Everything is a tour de force. He turns a toy into an instrument of shocking impact, urging from it a collection of sound equal to half an orchestra."
Newsweek

"His tongue-twisting technique and feathery phrasing have dazzled concert audiences..."
Time

With the Mercury Award to recognise sales in the UK of more than 100,000 copies of *The Glory of Gershwin*.

Recording with Sir George Martin and Cher

Larry Wallbanger, his martini. Martini's, London

At the book launch of *Morgan's Castle* with Dame Beryl Bainbridge and the author, Jane Huxley

With his editor at The Café Delancey, London

With Sting at
The Royal Albert Hall

Rehearsing with John
Ogdon, 75th Birthday
Gala Concert,
Royal Albert Hall